More BARBER SHOP HARMONY

A COLLECTION OF NEW AND OLD FAVORITES FOR MALE QUARTETS

EDITED BY
SIGMUND SPAETH

INDEX

Always a top favorite with male quartets . . .

the original

BARBER SHOP HARMONY

compiled and edited by Sigmund Spaeth

CONTENTS

**DINAH • GIRL OF MY DREAMS • MARGIE • THE LOST CHORD
I CAN'T GIVE YOU ANYTHING BUT LOVE • WAY DOWN HOME
BRIGHT WAS THE NIGHT • MY EVALINE • AURA LEE**

and many other famous songs.

Foreword by a PICK-UP QUARTET

Speaking as an average barber-shopper, I think this is a good book. Sig Spaeth's first folio of *Barber Shop Harmony* and his original *Barber Shop Ballads* were also good books. But this folio belongs more intimately to the Society for the Preservation and Encouragement of Barber Shop Quartet Singing in America. The arrangements represent some of our best known individual members and quartets. They have the full approval of the Arrangements Committee, of which I had the honor to be a recent chairman.

The Society appreciates the practical work of our New York member in editing these collections and gives hearty thanks also to the composers and arrangers who have so generously contributed their services. Having acted as Emergency Tenor in something over 2000 catch-as-catch-can sessions, I deeply appreciate this book as a record of inestimable value to other emergency as well as full-time tenors, not to speak of the three lower voices.

—*Phil Embury, Emergency Tenor and President, SPEBSQSA*

Parenthetically, when this folio was started, my job was the Lead, and it is still a pleasure to have the harmonious co-operation of Phil Embury, Sig Spaeth, Deac Martin and many others in the significant cause of *Barber Shop Harmony*. The literature on that important subject is rapidly growing, and in this case we have a real contribution by the Society itself. All of our members, as well as those who are still on the outside, are sure to welcome so stimulating a selection of typical material. If there is any doubt as to how the Lead was sung by such-and-such a quartet, here it is on the record for "swiping" by other fours, anywhere. May the "swipes" be frequent and enthusiastic.

—*Hal Staab, Lead and Immediate Past President, SPEBSQSA*

Everybody has been so helpful in getting together this book that the official Editor almost had little else to do except seeing to it that it was properly published and distributed. Naturally space limitations prevented our including all the songs we would have liked to, and already it is apparent that a third volume will be needed in time.

More Barber Shop Harmony represents a cross-section of what is regularly sung by the quartets of SPEBSQSA and therefore a model for all harmonizers of the barber shop school. The arrangements are by practical men, unhampered by technical formulas but well aware of how these highly individual effects can be made to *sound*. Experts will realize that much of this material goes far beyond the conventional barber shop harmony of the past. In only a few cases has it seemed necessary to make any concessions to average vocal abilities. As one who, throughout a long life, has experimented with all four parts, meeting even the challenge of the Baritone, I am delighted to know at last how the *real* Baritones do it.

—*Sig Spaeth, Editor and Rough and Ready Baritone*

Broadly speaking, my part is a minor one in this quartet. But since my blessing, for the Society, was on the first volume, I want to repeat it *fortissimo* herewith. Having grown up with barber shop harmony, and written a few things about it myself, I can appreciate what it means to have all these brains and voices collaborating so successfully to establish our ideas and ideals in a permanent form. Personally I want to serve notice on all the so-called Bass singers in the Society (including Frank Thorne, Gordon Hall, Fred Stein, Tommy O'Heren, Fred Graves, Johnny Buitendorp, Joe Wolff, Pete Buckley and Squire Barber) that they are going to be out of a job when I learn their parts out of this book.

—*Deac Martin, Past Historian, Ex-Vice-President and Tentative Bass*

More BARBER SHOP HARMONY

All Through The Night

Words by H. Boulton
As sung by
The Ramblers,
Cleveland, Ohio

Welsh Melody
Arranged by Sigmund Spaeth

11314

c/o CPP/BELWIN, INC., Miami, Florida 33014

In The Gloaming

Words by Meta Ored
As sung by
The Four Mugs, Detroit, Mich.

Music by
Annie F. Harrison
Arranged by Phil Embury

In the gloam-ing, oh, my darl-ing! When the lights are dim and low,
Think not bit-ter-ly of me!

And the qui-et shad-ows fall-ing, Soft-ly come and soft-ly go,
Tho' I pass'd a-way in si-lence, Left you lone-ly, set you free,

When the winds are sob-bing faint-ly With a gen-tle un-known woe,
For my heart was crush'd with long-ing; What had been could nev-er be.

Will you think of me and love me, As you did once long a-go?
It was best to leave you thus, dear, Best for you and

me;__ It was best to leave you thus,__ Best for you and best for me.__

Nelly Was A Lady

As sung by
The Hard-Rock Harmony Four,
Reno, Nevada

Words & Music by
Stephen Collins Foster
Arranged by Charles M. Merrill

11314

Nobody's Sweetheart

As sung by
The Elastic Four, Chicago, Ill.

By Gus Kahn, Ernie Erdman
Billy Meyers & Elmer Schoebel
Arranged by Frank H. Thorne

You're no-bod-y's sweet-heart now, ___ They don't ba-by you some-how. ___ *(And with your)* Fan-cy hose, ___ *(Your brand new)* silk-en gown, You'd be out of place in your own home town. When you walk down the av-e-nue, ___ I just can't be-lieve that it's you. ___ Paint-ed lips, ___ paint-ed eyes, ___ Wear-ing a bird of Par-a-dise. ___ It all seems wrong some-how, ___

Tell Me Why

As sung by
The Western New Yorkers, Warsaw, N.Y.

Old Song arranged by
Phil Embury

11314

While Strolling Through The Park One Day

As sung by
The Forest City Four,
Cleveland, Ohio

Words & Music by Ed. Haley
Arranged by Phil Embury

Coney Island Baby

As sung and arranged by
The Mainstreeters, Tulsa, Okla.

CHORUS

Oh, Good-bye, my Con-ey Is-land Ba - by, Fare-well my own true

love, true love. I'm gon-na go a-way and leave you, Nev - er to see you an-y,

my hon-ey,

I'm goin' to sail up-on that fer - ry boat,

Nev- er goin' to see you an-y,

Nev - er to re-turn a - gain. re-turn a-gain. So good-bye, fare-well,

re - turn a - gain.

So-long for ev- er, Good-bye, my Con- ey Isle, Good-bye, my Con- ey Isle,

Boom - boom, _____ De - Hi, _____ De-
Boom - boom, _____ Boom - Boom, _____ Me-

Good-bye, my Con - ey Is - land Babe.

(To Verse) Last time only

Ho!
ow!

Bye, my Con - ey Is - land Babe.

Fine

VERSE

We all fall for some girl that dress-es neat Some girl that's got big feet,

We meet her on the street; Then we'll join the ar-my of mar-ried boobs,

To the al-tar, When it's o - ver,

Just like lead-ing lambs to slaugh-ter.

Oh boy we get it good, Bach-'lor days we then re - call. we then re-call.

we then re-call.

Rich man, poor man, beg-gar man, thief, Doc-tor, law-yer, mer-chant chief, We all are bound for

11314

D. S. al Fine

Bye-Lo

As sung by
The Cessna-Aires, Wichita, Kansas

Words & Music by
Ray Perkins
Arranged by Dean Palmer

Bye - lo, your eyes are clos - in', hon - ey,

Bye - lo, you'll soon be doz - in', hon - ey, Oh, — my —

lit - tle stick of eb - o - ny, your mam-my's by your side.

Bye - lo, you're tired of play - in' hon - ey, Bye - lo,

— your head is sway-ing, hon - ey. Time — to — take the train to slum-ber land,

The sand-man's com-in', your dad-dy's strum-min', your mam-my's hum-min'. Good-
Oh, your dad - dy, your mam - my.

Bye - lo, my ba-by's go-in' to sleep.
Bye - lo, Bye - lo,
Bye - lo, Bye - lo,

Shine On Me

As sung by
The Lamplighters, Cleveland, Ohio

Arranged from an old Hymn
By Deac Martin

Shine on me (in the morn-in') Shine on me, Will the light in the

light-house shine on me? Shine on me (in the ev'-nin')

Shine on me, I won-der if the light-house, will shine on me.

11314

Down Among The Sugar Cane

Written by Avery & Hart
As sung by The Harmony Halls,
Grand Rapids, Mich.

Composed by Cecil Mack &
Chris Smith
Arranged by Phil Embury

Moonglow

As sung by
The Four Flats,
Cleveland, Ohio

Words & Music by Will Hudson,
Eddie De Lange & Irving Mills
Arranged by Don Webster

It must have been Moon - glow, _____ Way up in the

Boom, Boom, Boom, Boom, Boom, Boom, Boom, Boom, Boom, Boom,

blue, It must have been Moon - glow

Boom, Boom, Boom, Boom, Boom, Boom, Boom, Boom, Boom, Boom, Boom, Boom,

that led me straight to you; I still hear you

Boom, Boom, Boo, Boo, Boom, Boom, Boom, Boom, Boom,

say - ing: (Hum _____) "Dear me, hold me fast."

Boom, Boom, Boom, Boom, Boom, Boom,

And I start in pray - ing (Hum _) Oh Lord, please let this last.

Boom, Boom, Boom, Boom, Boom, Boom, Boom, _____ Boom,

c/o CPP/BELWIN, INC., Miami, Florida 33014

Violets Sweet

As sung by
The Tom Cats, Massilon, Ohio

Word & Music by
Hal Staab
Arranged by Frank H. Thorne

Vi - o - lets sweet, fresh with the dew, Vi - o - lets sweet_ for you.____ Flow'rs that grow in the spring - time, When ev - 'ry heart beats true._____ Oft in the ev'ning when we're a - part, Mem - o - ries lin - ger of you, dear heart. Vi - o - lets sweet, fresh with the dew, Vi - o - lets sweet_ for you.____

In The Fields Of Oklahoma

As sung by
The Unheard-of Four,
Muskegon, Mich.

Words & Music by Hal Staab
Arranged by Frank H. Thorne

Mister Moon

As sung by
The Hard-Rock Harmony Four,
Reno, Nevada

Adapted and arranged by
Charles M. Merrill

By the light of the moon, of the sil - ver - y moon, By the

bright shin - ing light, by the light of the moon; If you

want to go a - bar - ber - shop - ing, come a - long with me, By the

bright, shin - ing light of the moon, of the moon. Oh, Mis - ter

Moon, moon, bright and sil - v'ry moon, Won't you please shine down on

That Tumble-Down Shack In Athlone

Words by Richard W. Pascoe
As sung by
The Four Harmonizers, Chicago, Ill.

Music by Monte Carlo & Alma Sanders
Arranged by Maurice E. Reagan

Daddy, Get Your Baby Out Of Jail

As sung by
The Serenaders
Kansas City, Mo.

Words & Music by
Joe. E. Stern
Arranged by the composer

Copyright © 1944 by Mills Music, Inc.
This arrangement Copyright © 1945 by Mills Music, Inc.
International Copyright Secured   Made In U.S.A.   All Rights Reserved

c/o CPP/BELWIN, INC., Miami, Florida 33014

My Mother's Rosary

*As sung by
The Misfits, Chicago, Ill.*

Words by Sam M. Lewis
Music by George W. Meyer
Arranged by Ellis V. ("Cy") Perkins

It takes an old time love song To keep this old world young,

Each heart must have a love song, Though some are nev - er sung.

Some peo-ple wor-ship mon-ey, The sound of clink-ing gold.___

But moth-er's song at 'twi - light Bring you right back to the fold.___

CHORUS

There's an old time mel-o-dy_ I heard long a-go,____ Moth-er called it the

Mood Indigo

*As sung by
The Elastic Four,
Chicago, Ill.*

Words & Music by Duke Ellington
Irving Mills & Albany Bigard
Arranged by Frank H. Thorne

You ain't been blue,___ No, No, No,

Boom, Boom, Boom, Boom, Boom, Boom, Boom, Boom, etc.

You ain't been blue,___ Till you've had_ that mood in-di-go,

mood in-di-go,

That feel-in' goes steal-in' down to my shoes, While

Boom, Boom, Boom, Boom, Boom, Boom, Boom, Boom, etc.

To next strain

I sit and sigh ___ "Go 'long blues.___

blues.___

Last time only

blues, blues, blues, blues, mood in-di-go blues.

Fine

Boom, Boom, Boom, Boom, Boom, Boom, Boom, Boom, mood in-di-go blues.

We've Never Been Defeated In The U.S.A.

As sung by
The Peach Pickers, Atlanta, Ga.

Words & Music by
Richard H. Sturges
Arranged by Phil Embury

For we are proud to say That we are liv-ing in the U. S. A.

And that we're giv-ing all the help that's need-ed To fin-ish the scrap, With the

Gosh darn Na-zi and the dir-ty old Jap.— And when we've won the war,

With peace com-plet-ed, the mis-takes of yore Won't be re-peat-ed and the

rit.

world will say We've nev-er been de-feat-ed in the U. S. A.

11314

Notes

Notes

Notes

Notes